Documentary Portrait of Mississippi:
The Thirties

Documentary Portrait of Mississippi: The Thirties

Patti Carr Black EDITOR

UNIVERSITY PRESS OF MISSISSIPPI Jackson

Walker Evans. Hitchhikers, Vicksburg (vicinity). March, 1936.

Contents

Dorothea Lange. A cotton sharecropper's family, Cleveland (vicinity). June, 1937.

Introduction

The word "documentary" puts me off a little bit...
I'm interested in realism the way Flaubert was, and
I don't think you would call him a social documentarian.
I don't want to be called that either. I don't think
that's art. What I'm really interested in is art and
being an artist.

Walker Evans
to Bill Ferris, 1974

Despite the disclaimer, Walker Evans and his colleagues, Dorothea Lange, Russell Lee, Arthur Rothstein, Ben Shahn, and Marion Post Wolcott, photographers for the Farm Security Administration, introduced a way of seeing and a commitment that put the word **documentary** into the lexicon of serious photography.

The Farm Security Administration was a program of the New Deal, established to administer rural relief during the Great Depression. Begun in 1935 as the Resettlement Administration, it was renamed Farm Security Administration in 1937 and continued its work until 1943. During the agency's first year, Roy Stryker set up the now famous "historical section" under the Information Division. He hired several exceptionally talented photographers to cover the agricultural regions of the South, Midwest, Plains, and far West. Their initial assignment was to "record the performance of the agency" and to make photographs that would underline the need for FSA. Inevitably, as they traveled around the countryside, they began to record extraneous things: places and people that interested them, moved or amused them. Perhaps because of these qualities in the photographs being sent back to Washington, Stryker broadened his concept. By 1938 his intention was to document the entire rural background in which federal programs operated. The result was an unforgettable portrait of America during one of its most difficult decades.

It has been said that Mississippians felt the Depression less than the rest of the nation because they had so little to lose. Statistics tell a different story. By 1932 Mississippi's economy was totally devastated, with a per capita income of $126 and a bankrupt state treasury. Cotton, for many the only source of jobs and income, plummeted in price and crop yields faltered in the years 1930, 1931, 1932. While 225,000 tenant farmers struggled for subsistence, thousands of property owners lost their homes, businesses, and land. On a single day in April 1932, one-fourth of all Mississippi land was auctioned for unpaid taxes. Such conditions led to the creation of the Resettlement Administration, later FSA, which began work in Mississippi immediately.

The first FSA photographer to arrive in Mississippi was Arthur Rothstein, also the first photographer employed by FSA. He made brief visits to Lee, Pike, and Lauderdale counties in August 1935, recording living conditions on farms. Later that year, in October, Ben Shahn arrived in Natchez. A painter and lithographer, Shahn was not officially employed by the historical section. He traveled around to view the work of the agency and to take photographs for use as reference in painting murals and posters for the Resettlement Administration. His photographs of Natchez preserve ephemeral images of a small town in Depression Mississippi.

Walker Evans worked in Mississippi before joining James Agee in Alabama to collaborate on **Let Us Now Praise Famous Men.** As an artist called "senior information specialist," he largely ignored the agency's directives. Stryker sent instructions to Evans at the Carroll Hotel in Vicksburg in March, 1936:

> Put quite a little effort in getting us good land pictures, showing the erosion, sub-marginal areas, cut-over land. These should be taken wherever possible, showing the relationship of the land to the cultural decay. Cotton planting is probably now going on. Try to get us a few nice "sirupy" pictures of agricultural scenes and general landscape pictures for cover pages.

Evans, however, had other ideas. In the last interview of his life, he described to Bill Ferris his work for the FSA:

> I was going around on my own very freely, and wherever I pleased, just documenting the things that I saw and was interested in. All alone most of the time. I wasn't looking for anything; things were looking for me, I felt — just calling to me. I had an eye and a sense of regional atmosphere, and I automatically recorded it.

The photographs taken by Evans in Mississippi confirm his "eye and sense of regional atmosphere."

One of the most socially committed photographers was Dorothea Lange, who worked in Mississippi in the summers of 1936 and 1937. Dedicated to the cause of the rural poor, Lange had already gained a reputation for spotlighting the problems of migrant labor in California. Her assignment in Mississippi was to document tenant farming, primarily in the Delta, and her work there deals with people and the effect of poverty on their lives. A letter from Greenville, dated June 23, 1937, expressed her concerns.

Many, many tenant houses are vacant wherever you go. The change seems to be coming so fast. The Tenancy bill and its provisions is coming along late, maybe too late. . .

Russell Lee's major Mississippi assignment was the documentation of a cotton mill operation in Laurel, a city whose slogan, "the Chemurgic City," intrigued him. Writing from Hotel Pinehurst in Laurel, November 15, 1938, Lee reported:

Have just completed the first day's work at Laurel. The process is very interesting but the process of manufacture in step by step procedure may be slightly dull in pix. There is very little human activity as the plant is so highly mechanized.

His more memorable photographs were taken when he was "able to visit four or five families in the county and get a few shots of Saturday in Laurel."

The youngest of the photographers to come to Mississippi was Marion Post Wolcott, who joined FSA just as the focus of the work was shifting. After the summer of 1938, Stryker instructed his photographers to record a more balanced and complete picture of American life. This new directive probably accounts for the larger number and diversity of photographs taken by the younger photographer. Marion Post, a well-educated New Yorker, seemed to have an immediate affinity for the images and people of rural areas. She traveled through the Mississippi Delta in the fall of 1939 and returned in the summer of 1940 to drive down the river road to Rodney, Port Gibson, and

Natchez. Her photographs make up the bulk of the Mississippi collection and provide the greatest variety of material. She was the only photographer to try the new color film in Mississippi.

World War II ended Stryker's extraordinary photo-documentary project. As the Office of War Information absorbed the historical section, Stryker succeeded in transferring the FSA negatives to the Library of Congress for safe-keeping. Only a fraction of the approximately 140,000 black and white negatives and 1,600 color transparencies has been published. This compilation is the first attempt to present Mississippi through the eyes of the FSA photographers.

These images, along with Eudora Welty's **One Time, One Place,** help define for us the meaning of the Depression in Mississippi. They also may help others understand an observation that Walker Evans made shortly before his death: "I can understand why Southerners are haunted by their own landscape and in love with it."

Patti Carr Black

Arthur Rothstein

Arthur Rothstein. Sharecropper's daughter, Lauderdale County. August, 1935.

9

Arthur Rothstein.   Picking cotton, Lauderdale County. August, 1935.

Arthur Rothstein.   Sharecropper, Lauderdale County. August, 1935.

Arthur Rothstein. Picking cotton, Pike County. August, 1935.

Arthur Rothstein. Dogtrot, Lauderdale County. August, 1935.

13

14

Arthur Rothstein.   Wife and child of Negro sharecropper, Lee County. 1935.

Arthur Rothstein. Family in a wagon, Lee County. August, 1935.

Arthur Rothstein. Sharecropper's son, Lauderdale County. August, 1935. Cotton picker, Lauderdale County. August, 1935.

Ben Shahn

Ben Shahn. Two Negroes with a load of furniture, Natchez. October, 1935.

Ben Shahn. The house of a Negro family, Natchez. September, 1935.

Ben Shahn. Store front, Natchez. October, 1935.

Ben Shahn.   Two Negro boys who do not have a home, Natchez.   October, 1935.

Ben Shahn. A horse and mule auction room, Natchez. October, 1935.

23

Ben Shahn.   A one-legged man sitting in front of a building, Natchez. October, 1935.

Ben Shahn. Two women walking along the street, Natchez. October, 1935.

25

Ben Shahn. Natchez children. October, 1935.

Ben Shahn. A Negro fitting his mule's harness, Natchez. October, 1935.

Walker Evans

Walker Evans.   *Detail of a Negro house, Tupelo. March, 1936.*

Walker Evans. Erosion, Tupelo (vicinity). March, 1936.

Walker Evans.   A Negro cultivating a field, near Tupelo. March, 1936.

32

Walker Evans. Ferry and river men, Vicksburg. March, 1936.

Walker Evans.   The homes of Negroes, Vicksburg. March, 1936.

Walker Evans. Negro children, Vicksburg. February, 1936.

Walker Evans.   Ferry landing, Vicksburg. February, 1936.

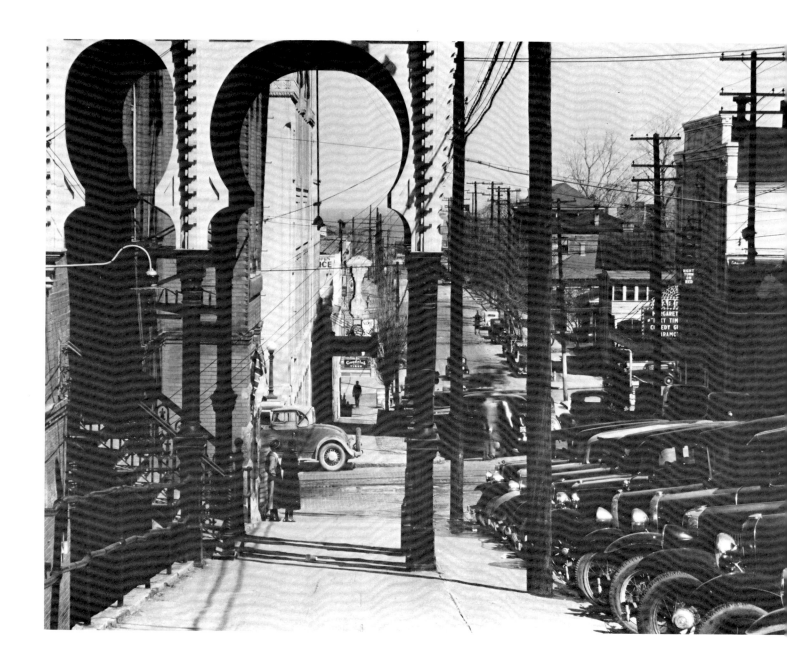

Walker Evans. A street scene, Vicksburg. March, 1936.

Walker Evans. Butcher sign, Vicksburg. March, 1936.

Walker Evans. Negroes in front of a shop, Vicksburg. March, 1936.

Walker Evans.   Commercial architecture of the 1890 period,
Vicksburg. March, 1936.

Walker Evans. Front of a general store, Edwards. March, 1936.

Walker Evans. View of a railroad station, Edwards. February, 1936.

42

Walker Evans. Store fronts on a main street, Edwards. March, 1936.

Walker Evans.   *Interior of a seed store, Vicksburg. March, 1936.*

Dorothea Lange

Dorothea Lange. A laborer, Issaquena County. June, 1937.

Dorothea Lange. A Negro woman hoeing cotton. She was born a slave two years before the surrender of the South, Clarksdale (vicinity). June, 1937.

Dorothea Lange. Sharecropper in a cotton field, Issaquena County. June, 1937.

Dorothea Lange.   A plantation owner, Clarksdale (vicinity). June, 1936.

48

Dorothea Lange. Cotton hoers who work from 6 a.m. to 7 p.m. for $1, near Clarksdale. June, 1937.

Dorothea Lange.   The wife of a sharecropper, near Clarksdale. July, 1937.

Dorothea Lange. Services for Negroes, Leland. June, 1937.

Dorothea Lange. Lunchtime for cotton hoers, Clarksdale (vicinity). June, 1937.

Dorothea Lange. The owner of the Aldridge Plantation with one of the plantation children, Leland (vicinity). June, 1937.

Dorothea Lange. Moving, Highway 1, Washington County. June, 1937.

Dorothea Lange. A grandmother of a sharecropper, Cleveland (vicinity). June, 1937.

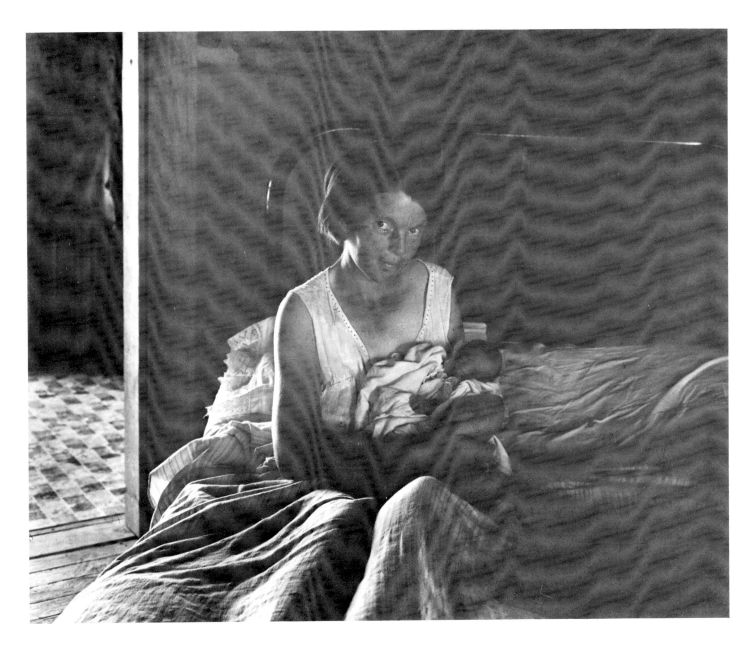

Dorothea Lange. A sharecropper's wife and her new-born child,
Cleveland (vicinity). June, 1937.

56

Dorothea Lange. 12-year old son of a sharecropper, Cleveland (vicinity). June, 1937.

Dorothea Lange.   Negroes working in a cotton field, Coahoma
County. June, 1937.

Dorothea Lange. Pressing cane for sorghum, Carthage (vicinity).
August, 1938.

Dorothea Lange. A sharecropper's cabin standing in a cotton and
corn field, Jackson (vicinity). June, 1937.

Dorothea Lange. Eating on a porch. Jackson (vicinity). June, 1937.

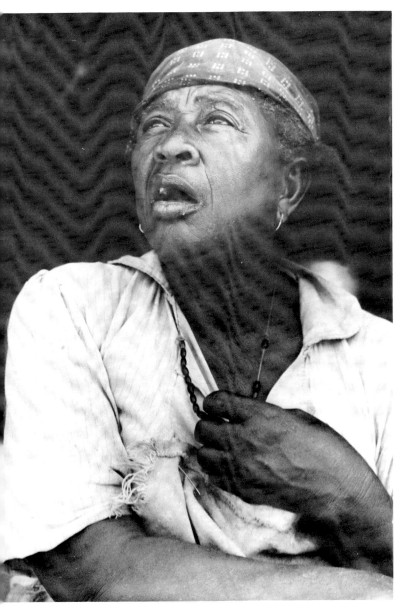

Dorothea Lange. 57 year-old sharecropper woman. She has black beads hung between her breasts as a remedy for heart trouble, Hinds County. June, 1937.

Dorothea Lange. A public library in the piney woods of the southwestern part of Mississippi. July, 1937.

Russell Lee

Russell Lee.   Row houses, Greenville. January, 1939.

Russell Lee. Sharecropper family, Pace (vicinity). January, 1939.

Russell Lee. Wife of tenant farmer, Pace. January, 1939.

Russell Lee. Son of a tenant farmer, Pace (vicinity). January, 1939.

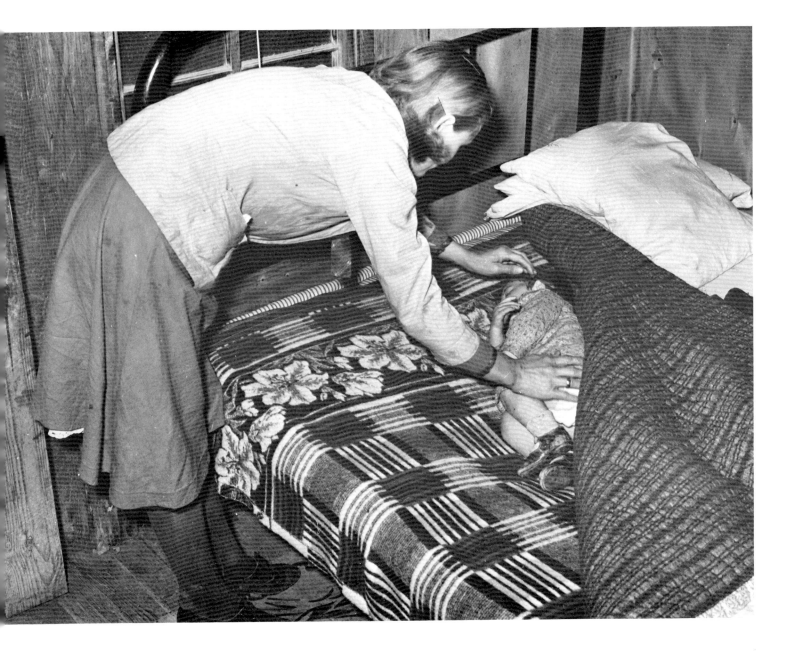

Russell Lee. Sharecropper's wife and child, Pace (vicinity). January, 1939.

Russell Lee. Quilting, Pace (vicinity). January, 1939.

Russell Lee. Farmers, Laurel. January, 1939.

Russell Lee. Cotton mill, Laurel. January, 1939.

Russell Lee. Family living in a church, near Pace. January, 1939.

Russell Lee. The Scarborough family, near Laurel. January, 1939.

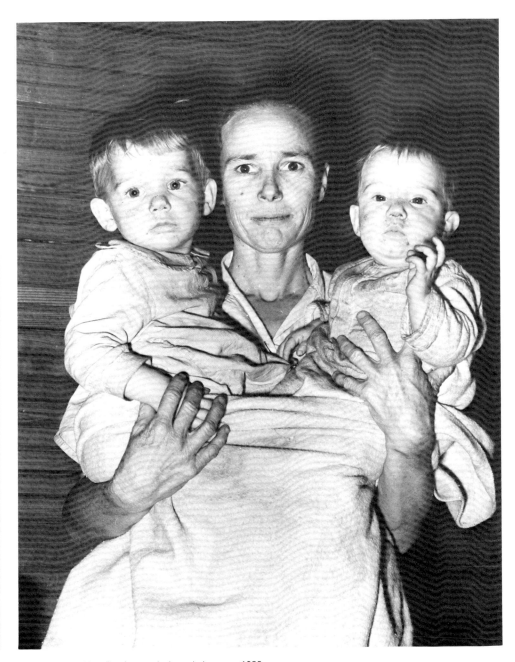

Russell Lee. Mrs. Scarborough, Laurel. January, 1939.

73

Russell Lee. Dogtrot, near Laurel. January, 1939.

Russell Lee.   Turpentine still, near Laurel. January, 1939.

Marion Post Wolcott

Marion Post Wolcott. A new hay rake, near Isola. November, 1939.

Marion Post Wolcott. Taking the cotton from the truck into the gin through a large metal suction tube, Hopson Plantation, Clarksdale. November, 1939.

Marion Post Wolcott. From the plantation to the warehouse, near
Clarksdale. November, 1939.

80

Marion Post Wolcott. A tourist court, Clarksdale. Everything is named "cotton-boll" in the Delta. October, 1939.

Marion Post Wolcott. Chitterlings, fish and sugar cane, Clarksdale.
November, 1939.

Marion Post Wolcott. Mexican laborers who were brought by a contractor to Hopson Plantation for the duration of the cotton picking season, Clarksdale. November, 1939.

Marion Post Wolcott. Jitterbugging in a juke joint on a Saturday
afternoon, Clarksdale. November, 1939.

84

Marion Post Wolcott. Saturday afternoon in a Negro beer and juke joint, Clarksdale, November, 1939.

Marion Post Wolcott. *Playing dominoes in front of the drug store, Tchula. October, 1939.*

Marion Post Wolcott. Itinerant salesman selling goods from his truck, Saturday afternoon, Belzoni. October, 1939.

Marion Post Wolcott. Bringing the cow from the fields, Belzoni.
October, 1939.

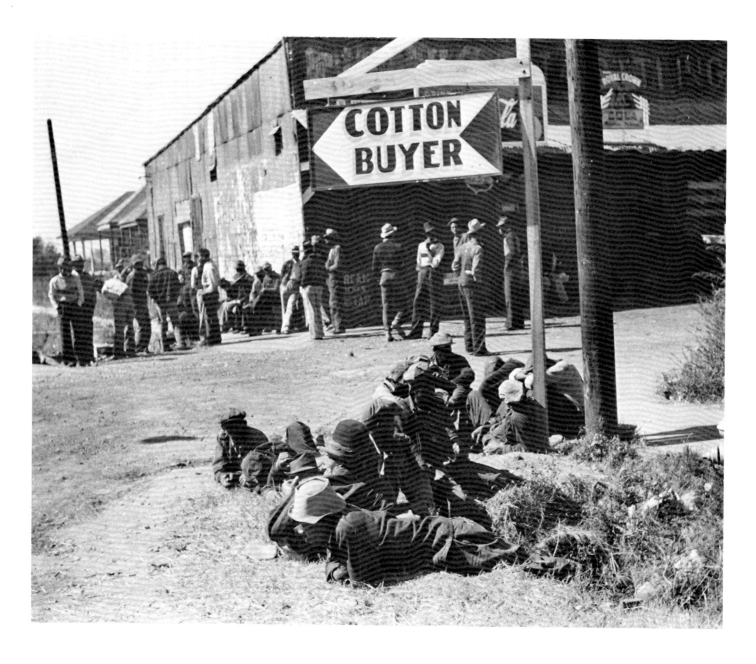

88

Marion Post Wolcott. The Negro section of town on a Saturday afternoon, Belzoni. October, 1939.

Marion Post Wolcott.   House interior, near Mileston. October, 1939.

Marion Post Wolcott. House interior, near Mileston. November, 1939.

Marion Post Wolcott. Rolling dice on a Saturday afternoon,
Marcella Plantation, Mileston. October, 1939.

92

Marion Post Wolcott. Cutting hair in front of the plantation store, Mileston. November, 1939.

Marion Post Wolcott. "Uncle George," blacksmith and carpenter on the Marcella Plantation for fifty years, Mileston. October, 1939.

Marion Post Wolcott. Business manager of plantation paying off cotton pickers on Saturday, Mileston. November, 1939.

Marion Post Wolcott.   Loading hay, Marcella Plantation, Mileston.
November, 1939.

Marion Post Wolcott. Post office inside the plantation store, Mileston. November, 1939.

Marion Post Wolcott.   Railway station, Mileston. October, 1939.

Marion Post Wolcott. Plantation store, Mileston. November, 1939.

Marion Post Wolcott. School room, Mileston plantation. November, 1939.

Marion Post Wolcott. A political poster on a sharecropper's house, Humphreys County. October, 1939.

Marion Post Wolcott. A grocery store operated by a Chinese,
Leland. November, 1939.

Marion Post Wolcott. The Rex theatre for Negro people, Leland. November, 1939.

Marion Post Wolcott. A street known as "Cotton Row," Leland.
November, 1939.

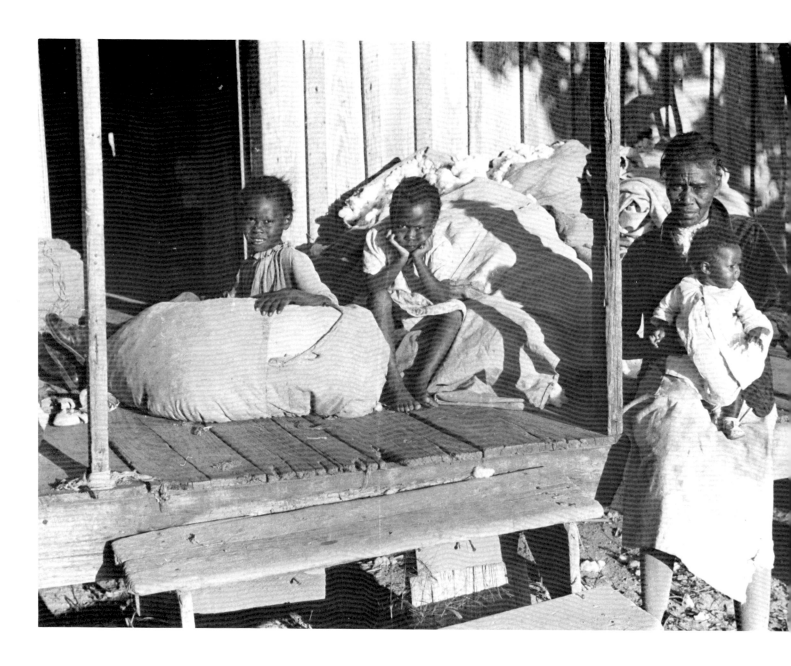

Marion Post Wolcott. A wage hand's family on the Knowlton Plantation, Perthshire. October, 1939.

Marion Post Wolcott. Tenant houses on a cotton plantation, Rolling Fork. May, 1940.

Marion Post Wolcott. Commissary, Sunflower Plantation, near Merigold. January, 1939.

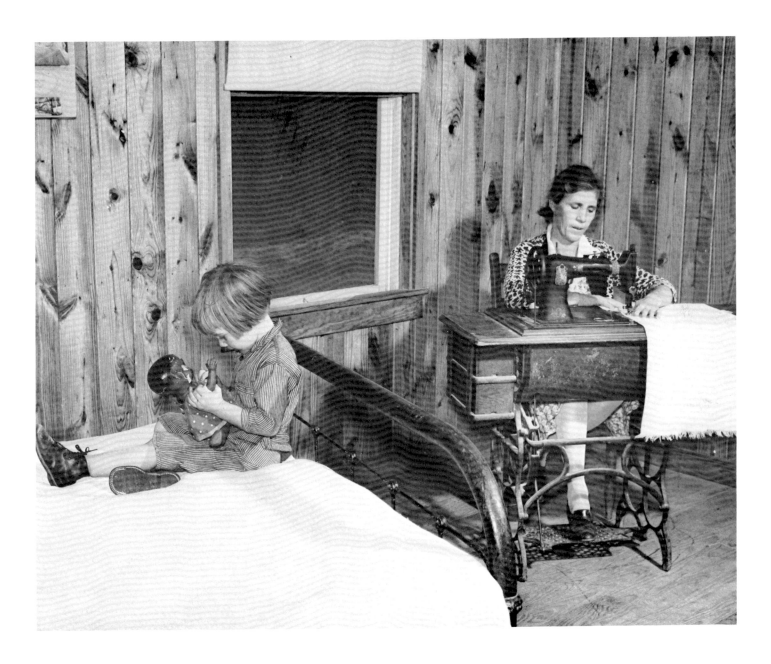

Marion Post Wolcott. *Woman and child, Merigold. January, 1939.*

Marion Post Wolcott. Selling fish on Saturday afternoon, Lexington. October, 1939.

Marion Post Wolcott. Visiting in front of the courthouse, Lexington.
October, 1939.

Marion Post Wolcott. Saturday afternoon in front of a cafe, Lexington. October, 1939.

Marion Post Wolcott.   A store front, Lexington. October, 1939.

Marion Post Wolcott. The courthouse steps, Lexington. October, 1939.

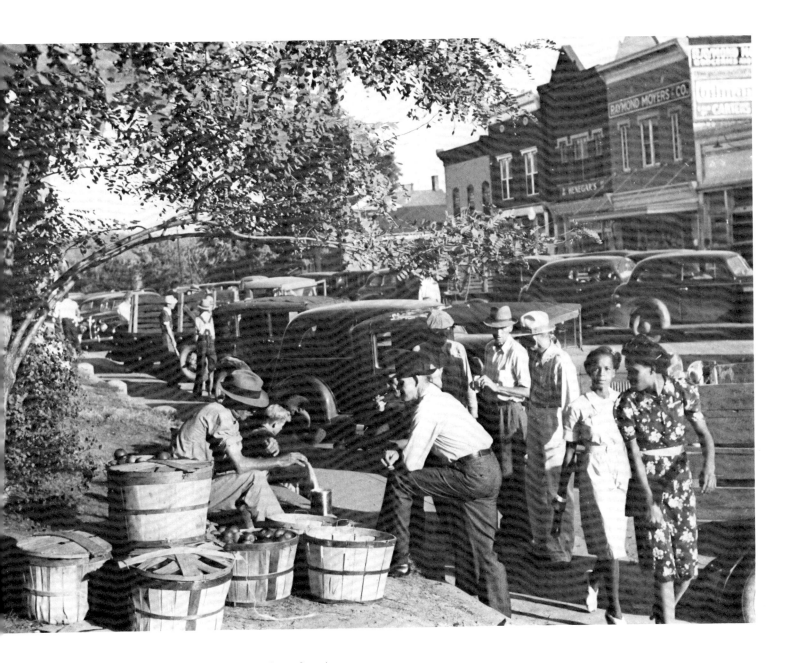

Marion Post Wolcott. *Selling apples on Main Street Saturday afternoon, Lexington. October, 1939.*

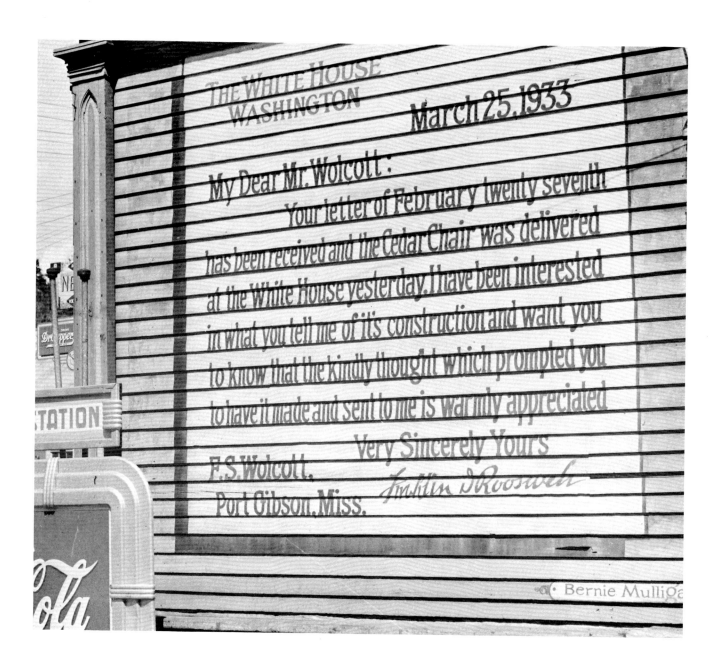

114

Marion Post Wolcott. Facsimile of a letter from FDR to a resident, Port Gibson. August, 1940.

Marion Post Wolcott. *A street scene, Port Gibson. August, 1940.*

Marion Post Wolcott. Carrying home supplies, Port Gibson. August, 1940.

Marion Post Wolcott. Two Negro women sitting outside an ice cream store, Port Gibson. August, 1940.

Marion Post Wolcott. Highway, near Port Gibson. August, 1940.

Marion Post Wolcott. Negroes sitting on the front of an inn, Port Gibson. September, 1940.

Marion Post Wolcott. Automobile decorated with "wise cracks,"
Rodney. August, 1940.

Marion Post Wolcott. Laborer, Natchez. 1940.

SURPLUS RELIEF COMMODITY
(NOT TO BE SOLD)
UNLAWFUL DISPOSITION OF THIS COMMODITY
PUNISHABLE UNDER THE LAWS OF EACH STATE
OF DISTRIBUTION

Marion Post Wolcott. A Negro woman carrying a bundle on her head, Natchez. August, 1940.

Marion Post Wolcott. A woman buying produce from a wagon in the street, Natchez. August, 1940.

Marion Post Wolcott.   A street scene, Natchez. August, 1940.

Marion Post Wolcott. A corner of a tree-shaded lawn, Natchez.
August, 1940.

Marion Post Wolcott. A street in the poorer section of town,
Natchez. August, 1940.

Marion Post Wolcott. A highway scene, Natchez. August, 1940.

This volume is sponsored
by the Mississippi Department
of Archives and History

Library of Congress Cataloging in Publication Data

Main entry under title:

Documentary portrait of Mississippi.

  1. Mississippi—Description and travel—Views.
2. Depressions—1929—United States—Pictorial works.
3. Mississippi—Social conditions—Pictorial works.
I. Black, Patti Carr.
F342.D62   976.2'062   82-4823
ISBN 0-87805-166-X   AACR2